OCHOSI

IFÁ AND THE SPIRIT OF THE TRACKER

AWO FÁ'LOKUN FATUNMBI
OMO AWO FATUNMISE, ILẸ́ IFẸ,
BABALAWO ÈGBÈ IFÁ, ODẸ RẸMO,
OLÚWO ILẸ́ ÒRÚNMÌLÁ OSHUN, OAKLAND, CA

Original Publications
22 East Mall
Plainview, New York 11803

© 1992 by Original Publications

ISBN: 0-942272-29-3

Cover illustration by *Awo* Fá'lokun Fatunmbi
Design and typeset by Royal Type

Printed in the United States of America

TABLE OF CONTENTS

ACKNOWLEDGEMENTS

The material in this book is primarily based on oral instruction from the elders of *Ifá* Ode Remo, Ogun State Nigeria and *Ilẹ̀ Ifẹ̀*, Oshun State, Nigeria. In appreciation for their time, patience and loving concern for my training and spiritual guidance I say: *A dúpé Ègbè Ifá Ode Remo, Babalawo* Adesanya Awoyade, *Babalawo* Babalola Akinsanya, *Babalawo* Saibu Lamiyo, *Babalawo* Odujosi Awoyade, *Babalawo* Olu Taylor, *Babalawo* Abokede Aralbadan, *Babalawo* Biodun Debona, *Babalawo* Oluwasina Kuti, *Babalawo* Afolabi Kuti, *Babalawo* Fagbemi Fasina, *Babalawo* Oropotoniyan and all the members of *Egbe Apetebi Ode Remo*.

Additional material in this book is based on instruction from the elders of *Ilẹ̀ Ifẹ̀*, Oshun State, Nigeria. In appreciation to them I say: *A dúpé Awon Ifá Fatunmise Ègbè Ifá Ilẹ̀ Ifẹ̀, Jolofinpe* Falaju Fatunmise, *Babalawo* Ganiyu Olaifa Fatunmise, *Babalawo* Awoleke Awofisan Lokore, *Babalawo* Ifaioye Fatunmise, *Babalawo* Ifanimowu Fatunmise, *Babalawo* Ifasure Fatunmise, *Babalawo* Adebolu Fatunmise and all the members of *Egbe Apetebi Awon Fatunmise*.

A special thank you to the members of *Ilé Òrúnmìlà Oshun* for their continuing support and understanding: *Olori Yeye Aworo Timi Lade, Apetebi Orunmila, Iya l'Orisha Oshun Miwa* (Luisah Teish), *Eko'fa Iya l'Orisha Omijinka, Iya l'Orisha Iya Oshun Iya Osogbo, Iya l'Orisha Shango Wenwa*, Leona Jacobs-White, Nzinga Denny, Earthea Nance, Vance Williams, Blackberri, Salim Abdul-Jelani, Rebecca Schiros, Carol Lanigan, Zena Attig, T'hisha, Rose Sand, Xochipala Maes Valdez, Dee Orr, Nina Heft, Ishoke, Luis Mangual and Earl White.

A final thank you to Maureen Pattarelli for her work in editing this manuscript.

Awo Fa'lokun Fatunmbi

INTRODUCTION

Ochosi is the Spirit of the Tracker in the West African religious tradition called *"Ifá."* The word *Ochosi* is the name given to describe a complex convergence of Spiritual Forces that are key elements in *Ifá* cosmology. Those Spiritual Forces that form the foundation of *Ochosi's* role in the Spirit Realm relate to the quest for balance between self and world. According to *Ifá* balance between self and world is the basis for the development of good character. It is the search for good character that serves as a basis for the *Ifá* concept of Destiny.

There is no literal translation for the word *Ifá*. It refers to a religious tradition, an understanding of ethics, a process of spiritual transformation and a set of scriptures that are the basis for a complex system of divination.

Ifá is found throughout the African diaspora where it spread as an integral part of Yoruba culture. The Yoruba Nation is located in the southwestern region of Nigeria. Prior to colonization, the Yoruba Nation was a federation of city-states that was originally centered in the city of *Ilę́ Ifę*. According to *Ifá* myth, the Yorubas migrated to *Ilę́ Ifę* from the east under the leadership of a warrior chief named *Oduduwa*. It is difficult to date the time of the Yoruba move into West Africa because of limited archaeological research on the subject. Estimates range from between sixteen hundred to twenty-five hundred years ago. It is likely that migration took place over a number of generations. As the population grew, each new city-state that became a part of the Yoruba federation was governed by a chief called *"Oba."* The position of *Oba* is a form of hereditary monarchy and each *Oba* goes through an initiation that makes them a spiritual descendant of *Oduduwa*.

Traditional Yoruba political institutions are very much integrated with traditional Yoruba religious institutions. Both structures survived British rule in Nigeria, and continue to function alongside the current civil government.

Within the discipline of *Ifá*, there is a body of wisdom called "*awo*," which attempts to preserve the rituals that create direct communication with Forces in Nature. *Awo* is a Yoruba word that is usually translated to mean "secret." Unfortunately, there is no real English equivalent to the word *awo*, because the word carries strong cultural and esoteric associations. In traditional Yoruba culture, *awo* refers to the hidden principles that explain the Mystery of Creation and Evolution. *Awo* is the esoteric understanding of the invisible forces that sustain dynamics and form within Nature. The essence of these invisible forces are not considered secret because they are devious; they are secret because they remain elusive, awesome in their power to transform and not readily apparent. As such they can only be grasped through direct interaction and participation. Anything which can be known by the intellect alone ceases to be *awo*.

The primal inspiration for *awo* is the communication between transcendent Spiritual Forces and human consciousness. This communication is believed to be facilitated by the Spirit of *Eṣu*, who is the Divine Messenger. Working in close association with *Eṣu* is *Ogun*, who is the Spirit of Iron. *Ogun* has the power to clear away those obstacles that stand in the way of spiritual growth. According to *Ifá*, the work done by *Ogun* is guided by *Ochosi*, who as the Spirit of the Tracker has the ability to locate the shortest path to our spiritual goals. The essential goal that *Ochosi* is called upon to guide us towards is the task of building "*ìwa-pèlé*," which means "good character." This guidance takes the form of a spiritual quest which is called "*iwákiri*."

The power of *Ochosi* is described by *Ifá* as one of many Spiritual Forces in Nature which are called "*Orisha*." The word *Orisha* means "Select Head." In a cultural context, *Orisha* is a reference to the various Forces in Nature that guide consciousness. According to *Ifá*, everything in Nature has some form of consciousness called "*Orí*." The *Orí* of all animals, plants and humans is believed to be guided by a specific Force in Nature (*Orisha*), which defines the quality of a particular form of consciousness. There are a large number of *Orisha*, and each *Orisha* has its own *awo*.

The unique function of *Ochosi* within the realm of *Orisha Awo* (Mysteries of Nature) is to find those pathways of inspiration that will lead to spiritual evolution. According to *Ifá* cosmology, spiritual evolution is in perfect harmony with the process of physical evolution that occurs in Nature. As a result, *Ochosi* has a twofold realm of responsibility. *Ochosi* both guides the development of personal spiritual growth and protects the needs of the environment. In order to do this, *Ochosi* must understand the inner dynamics of Nature so that human consciousness evolves in harmony with the physical world. In order to understand this relationship, *Ochosi* must be in direct contact with those Spiritual Forces who guide good character and those Spiritual Forces who maintain fertility and abundance in Nature.

At the core of *Ochosi's* power is the knowledge of the mysteries of plants. *Ifá* teaches that plants from the forest can be used for various forms of Spiritual cleansings. These cleansings form the basis for human access to communication with the Spirit realm. For this reason, *Ochosi* is known as the Magician of the Forest. It is through the use of herbal remedies, herbal charms and herbal baths that *Ochosi* is able to show us the vision of where we are headed, both individually and collectively. Because of this sacred responsibility, *Ochosi* is considered the Guardian of Forest. Those who unconsciously, or deliberately disrupt the balance of Forces that maintains life systems within the Forest will meet resistance to their efforts that are inherent within Nature itself. This resistance is identified as the power of *Ochosi*.

It is through the invocation of *Ochosi* that *Ifá* comes to understand the elemental spirits who preserve the balance of Forces that sustain life on the planet. *Ifá* teaches that all plants in the Forest have a form of consciousness. This consciousness takes the form of a group of Spirits which are called "*Irunmole*." The word *Irunmole* means "Light that comes from under the Earth." Light is used in the context of consciousness or illumination. The consciousness that guides such Forces of Nature as the Ocean are believed to be beyond human comprehension. However, aspects of the

Natural Forces can take on anthropomorphic forms which makes them intelligible to human understanding. In other words, the power of the *Irunmole* may present itself to human perception as a person or as an animal. When this power takes the form of an animal it is called an elemental spirit. According to *Ifá*, it is the elemental spirits who guide the growth of plants, maintain ecological balance between different species of animals and regulate the flow of the weather.

When interaction with the elemental spirits is needed, *Ifá* turns to *Ochosi* for guidance.

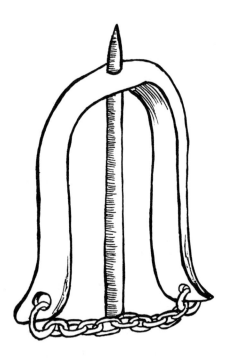

AŞẸ OCHOSI — altar piece for Spirit of the Tracker

I.

ALQ IRINTÀN OCHOSI
FOLKTALES OF THE SPIRIT OF THE TRACKER

A. *OCHOSI ÒDE MATA* — The Medicine of the Spirit of the Tracker

It was *Ochosi* (The Spirit of the Tracker) who scouted *igbó* (the forest) so that a path could be cleared by *Ògú* (The Spirit of Iron). *Ochosi* is known among the *Orisha* (The Immortals) as the greatest *ode* (hunter), because he has become *Osolikẹrẹ* (The Magician of the Forest).

Ochosi was the one who provided food for his family. *Ochosi* was the one who provided food for his extended family. *Ochosi* was the one who provided food for his village. *Ochosi* was the one who taught *awo 'de* (the mystery of hunting) to those whose destiny it was to track game in the forest.

The *aṣẹ* (power) to make *Ochosi* an effective hunter was kept by his pet *odidẹ* (the parrot). The spotted bird was called "*Odidẹ la ko gbo ògún*," which means "the parrot who collects the medicine used for hunting."

Before leaving the house, *Ochosi* also spoke to his pet saying, "*Odidẹ gan fi di ja*," which means "Parrot guide me beyond fear." *Odidẹ* (the parrot) was always the first to be fed when *Ochosi* returned from the hunt. On the day that the animals disappeared from the forest, *Ochosi* left his *odidẹ* in the care of *Iyagba* (his grandmother). In all the world *Ochosi* loved none more than *Iyagba*, and he knew that *odidẹ* would be safe while he was gone.

Heading out into *igbó* (the forest), *Ochosi* started searching for game. On the first day he found none. On the second day, he found none. A week passed without results. A month passed with no luck. Eventually he lost track of time. Rather than return home empty handed, *Ochosi* continued to travel deeper and deeper into *igbó*. All of his attention was concentrated on looking for signs as he hunted for food that would feed his family, food that would feed his extended family, and food that would feed his village.

On the day that he sighted *ekuté* (the bush rat), he placed *odidę mata ògún* (the parrot's medicine) on his arrow. When *odidę mata ògún* was in place, he used *ǫfǫ̀ aşę* (the power of invocation) to ask that his aim be true. *Ochosi* caught *ekuté* (the bush rat) with a single shot. Taking the animal by the tail, he hurried home to feed those who were waiting for his return.

When he arrived home he went directly to the cage of *odidę* to offer his pet some food. *Odidę* was not in the cage. All that was left of his pet were a few scattered feathers. In pain and anguish *Ochosi* ran outside crying for vengeance. He placed *ode mata odidę* on the tip of his arrow. When the medicine was secure, he used *ǫfǫ̀ aşę* (the power of the word) to invoke for his arrow to strike the person who had eaten *odidę*. *Ochosi* pulled back on his bow and shot the arrow high into the sky.

Ochosi went inside his house and found that his arrow had pierced the heart of *Iyagba* (his grandmother). From that day on those who worship *Ochosi* (The Spirit of the Tracker) praise him by saying, *"Iba a şę Òde ata mataşę,"* which means "I praise the hunter who never misses his target."

Commentary: In *Ifá* there is a proverb that says, "If it doesn't matter where you are going any road will do." This refers to all those who refuse to take seriously the question of finding your personal destiny. It is the function of *Ochosi* within the context of *Ifá* and *Orisha* ritual to lead us to the shortest route that will bring us in perfect alignment with our destiny.

This myth suggests that those who search for their highest path of destiny may be sabotaged by those who are closest to us. In the myth the grandmother eats the parrot because of personal need for food, completely ignoring the importance of the relationship between *Ochosi* and his bird. In *Ifá* the parrot is sometimes trained to say certain key words that are essential to *awo ǫfǫ̀ aşe* (the mystery of the art of invocation). By using an animal as an instrument of invocation, there is no risk that the intention behind the words spoken will be obstructed by inappropriate thoughts.

In this myth the parrot is the source of *Ochosi's aşę* (spiritual power), which suggests that *Ochosi* uses the *odidę* to prepare the medicine that he places on his arrow. His grandmother eats the parrot because of her immediate need, and this has a negative effect on *Ochosi's* ability to make medicine in the future. From a short-term ethical point of view, the need for food may have justified the actions of the grandmother, but it did not take into consideration the relationship between the bird and the hunter.

Ochosi's anger over this shortsighted indiscretion causes him to use his power against the unknown source of his anger. As he speaks the invocation, he feels that he is justified in his action. When he discovers who was responsible for the death of the parrot, he experiences deep grief. This suggests that the desire for justice does not always bring the desired result. *Ochosi* believed that the use of deadly force was justified given the circumstances, but he realized too late that he did not fully appreciate what had happened.

Because *Ochosi* is one of the key elements in placing individuals on their path of destiny, he has a pivotal role in enforcing justice against those Forces that block the process of spiritual transformation. It is *Ochosi* who brings us the truth regarding who it is that supports our growth and who it is who hinders our growth. *Ochosi* brings this truth no matter how painful it may be.

As the skilled tracker, it is *Ochosi's* role to know, understand and invoke the spirits of the forest as a fundamental factor in the process of living in harmony with the world. It is the ecological balance that occurs in Nature which effects the cycles of weather, the fertility of the soil, the quality of the air and the availability of game for food. Every ecological environment shows signs of stress, strain and imbalance long before potential hazards reach a crisis point. Drought is often the result in changing cycles of the wind, depletion of the soil is often the result the overgrowth of a particular plant, and pollution of the water is often the result of the improper use of natural resources. Each of these natural disasters give off signals which are easily noticed by the experienced tracker in the

African rain forest. When early warning signs occur, the elders of *Ochosi* are able to gather communal support of those efforts which will restore balance.

When *Orisha* was brought from Africa to the Western Hemisphere, it was the invocation of *Ochosi* that allowed *Orisha* worshippers to begin the process of spiritual alignment with those Forces that were present in the new environment. This would include giving respect to those ancestor spirits who originally lived on the land. Those Africans who preserved the mysteries of *Ochosi* during slavery began to study the wisdom of indigenous people so that they could establish the link between self and world. For this reason, *Ochosi* has come to be associated in the West with those Native American Spirits who serve as guardians of the land.

The oral history of African forms of spirituality that were brought to North and South America is rich with folklore telling of the interaction between slaves and the original inhabitants of the Western world. This history has been largely ignored by academic historians, but it remains an integral aspect of *Orisha* worship as it has survived in the diaspora.

B. *OCHOSI OLUWO IGBÓ NI* — The Spirit of the Tracker is Chief of the Forest

Qmọ Qbara was tending *oko* (farm) on the day that the *Qdẹ* (hunter) went into the forest searching for game. *Qdẹ* (hunter) traveled for days unable to find any game. In desperation he called to the *Oluwo Igbó* (Chief Priest of the Forest) pleading for help. As the *Oluwo Igbó* emerged from the brush, he asked *Qdẹ* why he was calling.

Qdẹ said, "I am in need of wealth, I am in need of abundance, guide me to the riches of the forest."

The *Oluwo Igbó* handed *Qdẹ* six pumpkin seeds and disappeared back into the forest.

Thinking that the seeds were some kind of magic, *Qdẹ* placed them in a sack and hurried home expecting the seeds to become transformed into jewels and precious beads. When he reached his village he opened his sack and was disappointed to discover that the seeds had not changed. In disgust he handed to seeds to *Qmo Qbara* who was still working on his farm. The seeds became pumpkins and the pumpkins produced more seeds and *Qmo Qbara* became a wealthy man by selling his goods at the market.

Qdę returned to the forest to look for the *Oluwo Igbó* to tell him that his magic had not worked and that he was still a poor man. *Qdę* searched and searched, but never again found the man who had given him the seeds.

Commentary: From a cultural point of view, this story is a commentary on the on the historical shift from a hunting culture to a farming culture that occurred in Yoruba society several thousand years ago. This shift in emphasis does not mean that hunters and trackers have an unimportant role in the overall stability of Yoruba communities. Most villages in the African rain forest still have societies of hunters and trackers who preserve the mysteries of *Ochosi*. It is the trackers who locate new parcels of land that can be used for farming. It is the trackers who gather the herbs that are used as elements of spiritual and physical healing. It is the trackers who monitor the conditions in the forest to warn the farmers of potential hazards. It is the trackers who locate new sources of game used to supplement the diet grown on the farm. In many communities it is *awon Ochosi* (society of trackers) who maintain the martial arts used to defend the village from invasion and intrusion.

Most towns in the portions of the rain forest that are populated by traditional Yoruba families, maintain shrines to *Eşu, Ògú* and *Ochosi* at either the entrance to the city or near the market place. These shrines are used as focal points for prayers and invocations that are considered essential for maintaining the peace and protection of all those who live in the immediate environment.

On a personal level, this story is a warning against the self-destructive consequences of egotism and self-centered expectations. The hunter asked the Chief of the Forest for the secret to riches and was given the punkin seeds. But the hunter had a very narrow expectation of the way in which he wanted abundance to manifest. As a consequence he spent the rest of his life searching for something that had already been given to him. From a historical point of view, most of the plants and animals that have become domesticated once lived in the forest as natural vegetation and as wildlife. At some point the worshipers of *Ochosi* began to bring back seeds from the forest, and they returned from the forest with animals that could be raised in captivity.

It was the preservation of these skills that allowed communities of escaped slaves to survive in the remote regions of Brazil, the Caribbean and portions of the Southern United States. Many of these communities existed for generations without contact from the outside world. The skills associated with *Ochosi* were put to use in a new and often hostile environment, which speaks to the tremendous depth of wisdom contained within *awo Ochosi* (the mysteries of the Spirit of the Tracker).

This story is taken from the *Odu* (verse of scripture) called *Qbara Meji*. In this instance *Ochosi* is described by his praise name "*Oluwo Igbó*," which means "Chief of the Forest." The role taken by *Ochosi* in this folktale is that of Magician of the Forest. A hunter comes into the forest looking for the key to unlock the mystery of abundance. When he is given the magic formula for creating abundance, he ignores it, assuming that magic should take some miraculous form involving instant solutions to the problem at hand.

Ifá scripture repeatedly states that transformation always takes place bit by bit, one step at a time in slow, steady increments. *Ochosi* is generally described as a person of patience and persistence. In the West, ritual magic is often viewed as an instantaneous fix to any problem. If their results are not immediate and miraculous, then it does not seem magical. *Ifá* takes the view that magic is the result of unshakable will and determination focused on the solution to a given problem. In order for this process to be effective, there must be a willingness to objectively evaluate and discard that which does not provide the desired result. *Ochosi* assists us in keeping our attention focused on the desired goal so that we can maintain our focus and attention on finding the effective solution.

The tracker who is hunting game in the forest often must sit for hours or days, remaining motionless in a single spot before he is able to snare his target. At times spiritual growth requires the same level of concentration, determination and patience.

C. *OCHOSI QDẸ* — The Spirit of the Tracker as Hunter

Orisha worship came to the West as a consequence of the slave trade. When Africans were forced to live in a new place, they were not only forced to abandon their culture, their religion, their family structure and their freedom, they were forced to live in an unfamiliar environment inhabited by unfamiliar Spiritual Beings. Because *Ifá* teaches that all things which exist in the world have *ori*, or consciousness, those who worshiped *Orisha* in the diaspora found it necessary to introduce themselves to the Spiritual Powers who animated the forests in the Western Hemisphere.

Among the Yorubas, the Spirit of *Ochosi* was invoked to gather the Spirits of the forest so that the *Orisha* worshipers could begin to establish a relationship with the indigenous Spirits of the land. In·conjunction with this spiritual process, those slaves who maintained traditional forms of spirituality developed close relationships with the Native religious teachers of both North and South America. As this interaction developed, *Ochosi* took on the characteristics of the indigenous people who lived in the West.

The interaction between African slaves and Native Americans must have been extensive, because it was this interaction that allowed *Orisha* worship to replace the traditional herbs and plants used in African ritual with the sacred fauna of the diaspora. This chapter of American history has been largely ignored by academic historians, but is evident in many of the spiritual retentions associated with *Ochosi*. One of the clearest examples of this interaction was among the Seminoles of the southeastern region of the United States. The Seminole Nation was made up of Native Americans who were fleeing from colonization and of Africans who had escaped the tyranny of slavery. Together they built a culture that survives to this day in the rural regions of Florida.

During the period of slavery *Ochosi* was one of many Spirits who were invoked for both protection and for guidance on the path towards liberation. In this historical context *Ochosi* was called upon to seek justice in response to unjust laws and an unjust social structure. *Ochosi* continues to provide this kind of guidance, but it is always done in the context of developing good character. This aspect of *Ochosi* is sometimes misunderstood. To suggest that simply making an offering to *Ochosi* will provide protection for engaging in any type of criminal activity is a blatant misconception. Such a misconception can have unwanted consequences. *Ochosi* gives guidance to those who seek spiritual growth; *Ochosi* does not provide protection for those who ignore the ethical principles of *Ifá*.

Because *Ifá* has no formal list of "ten commandments," there are those who argue that *Ifá* has no moral standards. This is an inaccurate assumption. *Ifá* scripture states clearly that everyone comes into the world with a deepseated sense of right and wrong. This inner sense is called "*èri-okàn*," which is usually translated to mean "conscience." A literal translation of *èri-okàn* would be "testimony of the heart." The word *èri-okàn* itself suggests that ethical behavior can be determined by making a close examination of inner feelings. According to *Ifá*, these inner feelings are an inherited aspect of the collective wisdom of both the ancestors and previous stages of reincarnation.

II.

ÌMỌ̀ OCHOSI
THE THEOLOGICAL FUNCTION OF THE
SPIRIT OF THE TRACKER

A. *OCHOSI ÀYÀNMỌ́-ÌPIN* — The Spirit of the Tracker and the Concept of Destiny

The *Ifá* concept of "*àyànmọ́-ìpin*," which means "Destiny," is based on the belief that each person chooses their individual destiny before being born into the world. These choices materialize as those components that form human potential. Within the scope of each person's potential there exists parameters of choice that can enhance or inhibit the fullest expression of individual destiny. *Ifá* calls these possibilities "*ọ̀na ipin*," which means "fate lines." Each decision that is made in the course of one lifetime can effect the range of possibilities that exists in the future, by either limiting or expanding the options for growth.

It is within the context of choice, or what is known in Western philosophical tradition as "free will" that *Ifá* recognizes a collection of Spiritual Forces called "*Ibora*." In Yoruba, the word *Ibora* means "Warrior." Traditionally, the *Ibora* include *Eṣu*, *Ògún* and *Ochosi*. *Eṣu* is the cornerstone that links the *Ibora* as they relate to the issue of spiritual growth. According to *Ifá* each moment of existence includes a wide range of possible actions, reactions and interpretations. Those moments which require decisive action are described in *Ifá* scripture as "*ọ̀na'padẹ*," which means "junction in the road." Whenever a person who is trying to build character through the use of *Ifá* spiritual discipline reaches *ọ̀na'padẹ*, it is custom-

ary to consult *Eşu* regarding the question of which path will bring
blessings from *Orisha.*

Ifá teaches that blessings come to those who make choices
that are consistent with their highest destiny. Within Yoruba culture
it is understood that an individual's highest destiny is based on those
choices that build "*ìwa-pèlé*," or "good character."

Once the road of good character has been identified it is the
function of *Ògún* to clear away the obstacles that exist along the
path of personal destiny. The role of *Ògún* as a warrior in this
context is to do whatever needs to be done to effect spiritual
transformation. In *Ifá*, when *Ògún* is invoked to remove obstacles
it is understood that those obstacles may be either internal or
external. Internal obstacles include fear, self-doubt, insecurity,
confusion, a lack of understanding, insufficient experience or improper motivation. External obstacles may include injustice, poverty, oppression, natural disaster, illness and misfortune.

One of the key issues associated with *Ògún* that arises during
divination is to identify the source of conflict. It is very common
for someone struggling with issues of spiritual growth to blame
external sources for what may be an internal problem. When this
occurs, the real issue is deflected and attention is given to solutions
that are doomed to failure because they ignore the root causes of
the difficulty in question.

Eşu opens the road of spiritual transformation, *Ògún* re-
moves the obstacles along the road, and it is the function of *Ochosi*
to locate and identify the shortest path between stages of development. It is the Spirit of *Ochosi* who goes to the heart of the matter
in question and gives us a clear image of the steps which must be
taken to overcome fear, limitation, restriction and cowardice. The
image of *Ochosi* alone in the forest hunting for game is a symbolic
reference to the human quest for guidance in the development of
good character. Each time an individual is faced with the dilemma
of finding the inner strength to make ethical choices, they are
thrown into the darkness of indecision, fear and confusion. The
path leading out of darkness is always one that is traveled alone,
but it is *Ochosi* who shows us the steps that must be taken.

B. *OCHOSI ONITOJU AŞẸ* — The Spirit of the Tracker as the Source of Guidance

Ifá cosmology is based on the belief that the Primal Source of Creation is a form of Spiritual Essence called "*aşẹ*." There is no literal translation for *aşẹ*, although it is used in prayer to mean "May it be so."

Ifá teaches that the visible universe is generated by two dynamic forces. One is the force of "*inàlo*," which means "expansion," and the other is the force of "*isokì*" which means "contraction." The first initial manifestation of these forces is through "*ìmo*," which means "light," and through "*aimoyé*" which means "darkness." In *Ifá* myth, expansion and light are identified with Male Spirits called "*Orisha'ko*." Contraction and darkness are identified with Female Spirits called "*Orisha'bo*." Neither manifestation of *aşẹ* is considered superior to the other and both are viewed as essential elements in the overall balance of Nature.

In *Ifá* cosmology both *ìmo* and *aimoyé* arise from the matrix of the invisible universe which is called "*Imole*," which means "House of Light." Within the house of light there is an invisible substance that transforms spiritual potential into physical reality. The invisible substance that moves between these two dimensions is called *aşẹ*, and it is *Eşu* who is given the task of guiding the distribution of *aşẹ* throughout Creation.

It is *Ochosi's* task to go out into the world and find that *aşẹ* which will be most effective in causing spiritual transformation for a particular person, at a particular time, in a given set of circumstances. It is *Ochosi* who locates the herbs that are used for physical healing by the priest of *Osanyin*. *Ochosi* also locates the medicine in the forest that is used for spiritual transformation by all the elders of *Ifá* and *Orisha*. On a practical level, it is *Ochosi* who locates game to provide food, new sources of water for irrigation and drinking, and it is *Ochosi* who reads the signs in Nature that predict sudden changes in the weather and the possibility of natural disaster.

In *Ifá* scripture *Ochosi* is known as "The Left Handed Magician." *Ifá* priests refer to the practice of magic as having two aspects which are designated as the "Right Hand Path" and the "Left Hand Path." The Right Hand Path is generally associated with practical or Earth related matters, while the Left Hand Path is generally associated with the realm of the invisible, or what is commonly called "Heavenly matters." The Yoruba word for magician is "*alafoşę*." This is a contraction of the words "ala," meaning "light" and "*afoşę*," meaning "power of the word." In English the word magician often has a negative connotation when used in reference to spiritual matters. However, the word *alafoşę* suggests one who uses the power of the word to manifest light. The word light in this context is synonymous with enlightenment.

As a magician, *Ochosi* is the guardian of those *awo* (mysteries) that bring instant transformation, instant changes in perception and the ability to penetrate to deeper levels of awareness. In *Ifá* myth, *Ochosi* is frequently associated with both *Ògún* and *Obatala*. The association with *Ògún* comes when *Ochosi* directs the power and strength of *Ògún* towards an elevated goal. The association with *Obatala* comes when *Ochosi* is guiding those who are confused towards clarity.

In Africa where hunters still travel into the forest in search of game, *Ochosi* worshipers preserve the *awo* (mysteries) associated with the poisons and charms used to track and capture wild game. This is an aspect of *Ifá* martial arts which is called "*Ijala*." The martial skills of *Ochosi* include hand to hand combat, the use of weapons, the knowledge of charms used for protection, and the use of charms that are used defeat an enemy.

It is in the area of the use of charms that *Ochosi* is frequently misunderstood and unfairly criticized. Many westerners who have no moral objection to the use of highly sophisticated laser technology during warfare are offended by the use of psychic skills in similar circumstances. *Ifá* would consider this to be an arbitrary distinction at best. Those who preserve the *awo* (mysteries) of *Ochosi* in Africa are considered the guardians of the *Ifá* discipline of martial arts.

In earlier times, many *Ochosi* worshipers would wear leopard skin when they went into the forest to hunt. The skin was both a form of protection and means of accessing the power of the leopard.

Ifá in Africa still makes use of animal and elemental spirits as allies in spiritual and survival matters. The ability to become possessed by the spirit of an animal is considered both a valuable learning tool and a way of enhancing ability as an hunter. This ability is the basis of most of the *Ifá* folktales about "shapeshifting," which means the ability of an animal to take on human form and the ability of an human to take on animal form. In the West, this aspect of *Orisha* worship has been diminished. The reason for this may be the lack of direct dependency on Nature for food and game.

III.

ÒNA OCHOSI
THE ROADS OF THE SPIRIT OF THE TRACKER

In Africa, the worship of *Ifá* and *Orisha* has a wide range of variation from region to region. Not all areas of Nigeria refer to the Spirit of the Tracker as *Ochosi*. In the Ijebu region of *Ògún* State the Spirit of the Tracker is called "*Lagua.*" In other areas the Spirit of the Tracker is closely associated with "*Erinle.*" Throughout Yoruba culture the names of historical figures who have been elevated to *Orisha* record the mythic exploits of famous hunters who have assimilated the characteristics of *Ochosi*. Within this spectrum of possibilities there are two fundamental roads or aspects of the Spirit of the Tracker. These roads include "*Ochosi Okunrin,*" which means "The Male Spirit of the Tracker," and "*Ochosi Obinrin,*" which means "The Female Spirit of the Tracker."

Again the role of each of these aspects of *Ochosi* shifts across the culture. In simple terms, *Ochosi Okunrin* explores the hidden mysteries of the physical world and *Ochosi Obinrin* explores the hidden mysteries of the inner self.

IV.

ILÉ 'BORA
THE SHRINE OF THE SPIRIT OF THE TRACKER

A. ILÉ 'BORA ADURA — Shrine for Prayer and Meditation to the Spirit of the Tracker

The religious symbols used to represent *Ochosi* include a bow and arrow, a hunting knife, and deer antlers. Those who want to pray to the Spirit of the Tracker as manifested in the West may use Native American symbols and images that honor the memory of those hunters and trackers who lived on this continent. This could include paintings, photographs or religious jewelry.

If you are setting up a shrine without the guidance of an initiated elder, use the shrine to pray for guidance, make *adimu* (food or drink) offerings, but do no invocations directly to *Ochosi*. The process of invocation should be done through the guidance of initiated elders. This is done both out of respect for the tradition and to avoid difficulties that can occur when you enter unfamiliar spiritual territory.

B. ILÉ 'BORA ORIKI — Shrine for Invocation to the Spirit of the Tracker

In the West, consecrated shrines for *Ochosi* take one of two forms. Most frequently a metal bow and arrow is placed inside a pot that is consecrated for *Ògún* (The Spirit of Iron). It is common practice in *Santería* and *Lucumí* to present *Eṣu*, *Ògún* and *Ochosi* together as a set. All three *Orisha* are usually placed near the front door of the house and used to invoke protection for the family and residence. At times divination will suggest that *Ochosi* should be placed on a plate next to *Ògún*. When this is done *Ochosi* usually includes a metal bow and arrow and deer antlers that have been prepared by an initiated elder.

Those who have a consecrated shrine to *Ochosi* may invoke the Spirit of the Tracker as follows:

> *Ìbá Ochosi.*
>> I praise the Spirit of the Tracker.
>
> *Ìbá olog'ararẹ,*
>> I praise the Master of Himself,
>
> *Ìbá Onibẹbẹ.*
>> I praise the Owner of the River Bank.
>
> *Ìbá Osolokerẹ.*
>> I praise the Magician of the Forest.
>
> *Ode ata matase,*
>> Hunter who never misses,
>
> *Agbani nijo to buru,*
>> Wise Spirit who offers many blessings,
>
> *Oni odẹ gan fi di ja,*
>> Owner of the parrot that guides me to overcome fear,
>
> *A juba.*
>> I salute you.
>
> *Aṣẹ.*
>> May it be so.

C. *ADIMU OCHOSI* — Offerings to the Spirit of the Tracker

In all forms of *Ifá* and *Orisha* worship it is traditional to make an offering whenever guidance or assistance is requested from Spiritual Forces. *Adimu* is a term that is generally used to refer to food and drink that is presented to the Spirit of a particular shrine. The idea behind the process of making an offering is that it would be unfair to ask for something for nothing. Those who have an unconsecrated shrine to *Ochosi* can make the offering in their own words. Those who have a consecrated shrine to *Ochosi* may use the following invocation:

Ochosi (name of food) *rę rę o.*
   Spirit of the Tracker we give you (name of food).
Fun wa ni alafia.
   Grant us peace.
Ma pa wa o.
   Do not cause us harm.
Gba wa lowo iku.
   Protect us from Death.
Ma je k'omo de re ewu oko.
   Protect our children from accidents.
Ochosi aladaameji t'o mu bi ina.
   I pay homage to the Spirit of the Tracker because he
   is worthy of respect.

Ochosi traditionally takes an offering of Anisette, corn, corn meal and palm oil.

D. *EBO OCHOSI* — Life Force Offerings to the the Spirit of the Tracker

Ochosi is traditionally feed in conjunction with *Ògún* and takes the same food as *Ògún*, depending on which road of *Ògún* the offering is being presented to. The following offerings are given to the specific roads of *Ògún*. When *Ògún* receives dog, it is in those areas of Nigeria where dogs are a part of the rural diet.

1. *alara* — dog
2. *onire* — ram
3. *ikole* — snail
4. *elemona* — roasted yams
5. *akirun* — the horns of a ram
6. *un* — tree sap
7. *oloola* — snail

Whenever a life force offering is made to any of the *Orisha*, an invocation is made to *Ògún* as part of the process. This is a grossly misunderstood aspect of *Ifá* and *Orisha* worship, which has suffered from negative stereotypes in the press and the media. It is part of *awo Ògún* (Mystery of the Spirit of Iron) to learn the inner secrets of making life force offerings. Part of the process involves the elevation of the spirit of the animal into the land of the ancestors and the request that the spirit of the animal return to Earth to continue its role in providing nourishment to the community.

When an *Orisha* initiate is making a life force offering it should include an invocation for the *Odu Ogunda*. If the initiate is using the *Lucumí* system of *Merindinlogun*, the invocation would be to *Ogunda Meji*. In *Ifá* the invocation for life force offerings is to *Ogunda-Irẹtẹ*.

E. ÀJABÓ OCHOSI — Charms for Protection with the Power of the Spirit of the Tracker

One of the aspects of *Ifá* and *Orisha* worship that is not well developed in the West is the use of *Ajabo* (charms) that are buried under the Earth. In Africa the construction of all *Orisha* and *Ifá* shrines involves the preparation of the ground itself. This usually involves burying certain elements and herbs that attract the presence of a particular Spiritual Force.

A common form of charm for protection that uses the power of *Ochosi* is to place an arrowhead in a small leather pouch to be worn around the neck. The arrowhead should be washed and cleaned in a bowl of water mixed with *efun* (sacred white chalk). Once it has been washed, *Osanyin* is prepared with the use of *Uniola virgata*, which is a member of the grass family commonly called "Sea Oats," or "*Espartillo*." The process for making *Osanyin* is the responsibility of an initiated elder who will know how to make use of the plant. After the second washing a prayer for protection is placed on the arrowhead as follows:

> ***Ochosi, olog'ararẹ,***
> Spirit of the Tracker, Master of Himself,
> ***Agbani nijo to guru,***
> Wise Spirit who offers many blessings,

Atoonalorogun odẹ ataparinyenku,
>   Mighty hunter who walks with pride,

Nle oo!
>   I greet you with respect.

Iba oooo ni ngof'ojo oni ju ooo.
>   It is with great respect that I say all of my prayers.

Ochosi mo ribaa, k'ibaa mi k'o moo se.
>   Spirit of the Tracker, I give you respect and ask that
>   my respect brings good fortune.

Ochosi, mo bo yin,
>   Spirit of the Tracker, I beg you,

Ma pa wa o.
>   Do not let me be harmed.

Gba wa lowo iku.
>   Protect me from Death.

Ma je k'ọmọ dẹ re ewu oko.
>   Protect me from accidents.

Ma jẹ k'agba ri aisan.
>   Do not let me suffer from disease in old age.

Jẹ ka ni alafia.
>   Bring me peace.

Aṣẹ.
>   So be it.

When the *ajabo* (charm) is prepared, divination should be done to determine if it is appropriate for the needs of the person who it is being prepared for. In addition, *Ochosi* should be asked if an offering to *Ochosi's* shrine is needed. The charm should sit in *Ochosi's* shrine for four days before being worn.

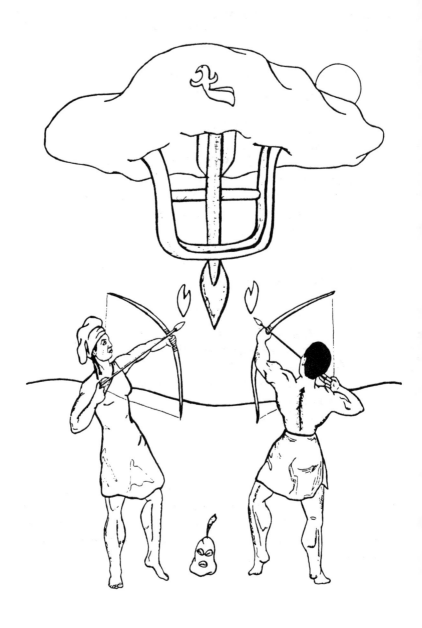

OCHOSI OBINRIN ATI OKUNRIN — female and male aspect
of the Spirit of the Tracker

V.

OCHOSI ONI'RE
THE SPIRIT Of THE TRACKER AS THE HUNTER OF GOOD FORTUNE

Ifá is based on the belief in *"Atunwa,"* which translates literally to mean "character comes again." This is a reference to the *Ifá* concept of reincarnation. It is the belief that the human soul (*èmí*) survives physical death and is reborn in the body of a newborn child. According to *Ifá*, *atunwa* occurs within a single family lineage. This means that a grandparent will return to life on earth as a grandchild.

Ifá also teaches that during the time between *atunwa* the *èmí* (human soul) resides in the realm of the ancestors which is called *"Orun."* While in *Orun* the *èmí* makes an agreement with Creation which establishes the lessons that will be embraced in the next stage of *atunwa*. This agreement is known as *"àyànmó̩-ipin,"* which means "Destiny." It is a fundamental belief of *Ifá* that Destiny is Character (*Àyànmó̩-ipin ni'wá*). In simple terms, *Ifá* is based on the belief that those who develop good character will receive the blessing of long life, abundance and children, while those who develop bad character will receive the curse of illness, poverty and infertility.

To say that *Ochosi* is the hunter of good fortune is to say that *Ochosi* is the Spiritual Power that can lead us to those character traits that will lead to a blessing from Nature Itself. *Ochosi* does not search for abundance based on greed, selfishness or egotism. *Ochosi* is first and foremost a guide who will keep us on the path of ethical behavior. Those who invoke *Ochosi* in a effort to avoid the consequences of those deeds which are based on unethical behavior are misunderstanding *Ochosi's* function in the world.

VI.

ORIN OCHOSI
SONG FOR THE SPIRIT OF THE TRACKER

Call: *Ochosi baba ayę.*
> Spirit of the Tracker, Father of the Earth.

Response: *L'odę ala mata odę.* (2x)
> The Hunter of the Medicine of Enlightenment.

Call: *Sirę sirę.*
> Bring good fortune, bring good fortune.

Response: *Odę mata orę orę.*
> Hunter of the medicine of kindness.

Call: *Sirę sirę.*
> Bring us good fortune, bring us good fortune.

Response: *Ode mata orę orę.*
> Hunter of the medicine of kindness.

Call: *Odedę odedę odedę.*
> Stand tall, stand tall, stand tall.

Response: *Odedę iwá lerę konfora.*
> Stand tall with the character of goodness.

ÒGÚN
Ifá and the Spirit of Iron
ISBN 0-942272-28-5 $4.95

Ògún is the Spirit of Iron in the West African religious tradition called *Ifá*. The essence of *Ògún* is considered one of many Spiritual Forces in Nature which are called *Orisha*. There are a large number of *Orisha* and each *Orisha* has its own *Awo*. The unique function of Ògún within the realm of *Orisha Awo* (Mysteries of Nature) is to remove all obstacles that stand in the way of Spiritual evolution, which includes the evolution of all that is. In order to do this *Ogun* must sacrifice all that stands in the way of spiritual evolution. Because of these sacred responsibility *Ogun* is considered the Guardian of Truth. *Ògún* does not protect the truth of what we would like to be, he guards the truth of what is. It is the process of making this distinction that lies at the core of *Ògún's* mystery.

This is the second in a series of booklets about the *Orisha*. Please feel free to write us and tell us which of the *Orisha* you would like to know more about.

Send your name and address to the address below and we will put you on our mailing list.

Send $2.00 for postage and handling and we will send you our latest catalog.

ORIGINAL PUBLICATIONS
22 East Mall
Plainview, New York 11803

OBATALA
IFÁ AND THE CHIEF OF
THE WHITE CLOTH

Obatala is the Spirit of the Chief of the White Cloth in the West African religious tradition called *"Ifá"*. The power of *Obatala* is described by *Ifá* as one of many Spiritual Forces in Nature which are called *"Orisha"*. There are a large number of *Orisha*, and each *Orisha* has its own *awo* (Mysteries of Nature).

The word *Obatala* is the name given to describe a complex convergence of Spiritual Forces that are key elements in the *Ifá* concept of consciousness. Those Spiritual Forces that form the foundation of *Obatala's* role in the Spirit Realm relate to the movement between dynamics and form as it exists throughout the universe. According to Ifá, dynamics and form represent the polarity between the Forces of expansion and contraction. Together these Forces create light and darkness, and it is *Obatala* who brings this into being.

This booklet is the fourth in a series of booklets on the *Orisha*. Write to us and let us know which of the *Orisha* you would like to know more about.

ORIGINAL PUBLICATIONS
ISBN 0-942272-29-3 $4.95

ESU - ELEGBA
***Ifa* and the Divine Messenger**

The Divine Messenger is generally known in Yoruba culture by the name *Esu*. Among those who practice Yoruba religion in the West, the Divine Messenger is commonly known by the name *Elegba*.

Esu is considered one of many Spiritual Forces in Nature which are called "*Orisha*". The word *Orisha* means "Select Head". In a cultural context, *Orisha* is a reference to the various forces in Nature that guide consciousness. according to *Ifa* everything in Nature has some form of consciousness called "*Ori*". The *Ori* of all animals, plants and humans is believed to be guided by a specific Force in Nature (*Orisha*), which defines the quality of a particular form of consciousness. There are a large number of *Orisha* and each *Orisha* has its own *awo*.

The unique function of *Esu* within the realm of *Orisha Awo* (Mysteries of Nature) is to translate the language of humans into the language of Nature, and to translate the language of Nature into the language of humans. The way in which this is done is the essence of the *awo* of *Esu*.

This booklet is the first in a series of booklets on the *Orisha*. Write to us and let us know which of the *Orisha* you would like to know more about the series.

32 pages; 5¼"x8¼"; paper $4.95

AWO
Ifá and the Theology of Orisha Divination
by Awo Fá'Lokun Fatunmbi

Throughout time people of diverse cultures have sought information to help them live their lives. Tarot, bone oracles, I Ching, playing cards, cola nut and tea leaves were among the sources consulted. The information obtained was used by the seeker to bring balance back into their world.

Within the Yoruba spiritual system the casting of sixteen cowries provides a finite tool that begins a transformation process that can lead to the healing of the seeker's concerns. Each throw of the shells brings forth an odu that begins to manifest immediately and continues as the diviner and seeker do the rituals the odu prescribes.

I have observed this process and its profound effect upon both diviner and seeker. For the diviner, there are always doors of knowledge being open through each reading that can lead to a deeper understanding of Orisha. The seekers learn how to develop spiritual balance as they work through their issues. Diviner and seeker can also experience their faith in action, bringing a deepening of their belief in Orisha.

Awo: Ifá and the Theology of Orisha Divination offers diviner and seeker a firm foundation in Yoruba divination. Also Awo reveals the Yoruba method of dilogun and gives initiated practitioners another way to use this oracle.

5¼"x8" 240 pages paper $12.95
ISBN 0-942272-24-2

Ìwa-pèlé
IFÁ QUEST
The Search for the Source of *Santería* and *Lucumí*
Awo Fá'lokun Fatunmbi

"*Ìwa-pèlé* blends belief and skepticism, intellect and emotion to give us the beauty of African mysticism and the power of western thought. Only a few white men have made a true effort to understand and embrace African Spirituality, Herskovitz, Griaule and Bascom. Now let us add Awo Fa'lokun." **LUISAH TEISH** *Author of, Jambalaya: The Natural Woman's Book of Personal Charms and Practical Rituals*

Ìwa-pèlé is an excellent introduction to *Ifá* religion. The modern Yoruba accent in this book has gracefully demonstrated Fatunmbi's remarkable talent for expressing quintessential African religion, which I agree to.

The taste of the pudding is in the eating.

Ire o. (Cheers) **ADEBOLU FATUNMISE**

5¼x8   214 pages Paper $11.95
ISBN: 0-942272-23-4